— Borderless —
—— Voice ——

THE POWER OF TELLING YOUR STORY
AND DEFINING YOUR IDENTITY

Chad   1-25-2020
The world is wanting for
your story!   GO.

Gbenga Ogunjimi

Design by Euan Monaghan.

Gbenga Ogunjimi
Visit my website at www.gbenga.org

Printed in the United States of America
First Printing: June 2018

ISBN-13: 978-1-7323911-0-9

Contents

"Voice is the manifestation of your life's purpose. This purpose can be expressed as a message, business, an assignment or a story. A Borderless Voice happens when these manifestations become completely unencumbered by any barriers. When you find your voice, you have found your purpose and that purpose has become the story you are now living to tell."

— BORDERLESS VOICE

I write this book on the shoulders of the heroes and heroines that have paved the way and blurred the borders that held many people back.

APPRECIATION

Thank you, Thomas Friedman for writing *The World Is Flat*, showing us there are no more geographical boundaries. I thank you Chimamanda Adiche for *The Danger of a Single Story*, telling us our story is our glory, and the world needs our stories to be a better place. I thank my social enterprise inspiration Ndidi Nweleli for the vision to create LEAP Africa, and Scott Beale, for creating Atlas Corps. It was in these organizations I found my voice as a social entrepreneur and changemaker.

Of course, I thank my many mentors, Cindy Trimm, Chris Abaga, Janet Feldman, Femi

Oye, Melissa G Wilson, and Segun Samuel Ogunjimi for helping to expand the parochial lens I had identified as my neighbor, build my tribe, and fulfill my responsibilities as a global citizen.

Special thanks to my editorial and research team, Erika White, Amy Lokoff, Nikita McRall, Leila Santos and Christina Chiu for your commitment to only allow the best ideas prevail.

Finally, I want to thank the amazing leaders whose stories I am telling in this book. Thank you for the opportunity to serve you as your life, story and identity coach.

FOREWORD

The concept of a *Borderless Voice* resonates strongly with me as an entrepreneur in the "identity business". AfricanAncestry.com is the pioneer of genetic ancestry tracing for people of African descent. Our mission is to transform the way that we view ourselves, and Africa. We do this through reconnecting Black people to Africa using their DNA.

When I first met Gbenga Ogunjimi, I did not know him as an Identity Strategist. I saw him as an international businessman who shared my passion for Black people knowing who they are by knowing first where in Africa they come from. He was excited about the impact of our work on all levels: personal, local, national and global.

Like the people whose stories are told in *Borderless Voice,* our clients are people who want to tell a different story. As the descendants of those who experienced the Transatlantic Slave Trade, we do not know where we come from beyond the shores of the Americas, the Caribbean or Europe. If we don't know where we are from then how can we know who we are? Tracing our family's ancestry back to present day African countries and ethnic groups removes the borders placed on how we see ourselves. We encourage them to explore their new found ancestry information and use it to craft and share a new personal story. Time after time we see that people have more pride, an inspired sense of belonging and feel much better about who they are when they know their roots. But that's just the beginning.

My favorite part of *Borderless Voice* is "The Power of Story". As an author, Gbenga Ogunjimi skillfully dissects the impact that story can have on building out one's identity. The stories that he shares illustrate how when you remove the limitations on how you see yourself and reframe your perspective, you instantly gain power. This power can be mental, intellectual, relational and/or spiritual and is wonderfully transformative.

I appreciate the authenticity and openness with which Gbenga Ogunjimi shares the power of having a Borderless Voice. The book is a practical and effective toolkit that will serve you well as you continue to evolve into your very best self!

Gina Paige
President and Co-founder
AfricanAncestry.com

Finding My Voice

The future is already here —
it's just not evenly distributed.

— *William Gibson*

IN THE 2001 MISS Universe Beauty Pageant, 19-year-old Miss Nigeria, Agbani Darego, became the first native African to claim the title of Miss World. It was a remarkable and unbelievable moment not just for Nigeria or the African continent, but for Black people around the globe. No black woman had ever made it that far in the competition, and yet, suddenly a teenage Nigerian girl had claimed a voice and identity for an entire race of people, giving them a sense of pride.

Then, a Nigerian business entrepreneur by the name of Ben Murray-Bruce put forth what seemed a laughable idea: that Africa could be a leader in the world of beauty. By global standards at the time, black was considered anything but beautiful. To some, Africa had produced little aside from the East African Marathoners and West African football (what Americans refer to as "soccer"), so when Agbani Darego was crowned Miss World, it was a resounding, universal victory for black people, who, until that moment, had felt invisible.

A second, coinciding event that put me on my journey to discovering my borderless voice was a TED Talk given by award-winning author Chimamanda Adichie at the TED Global gathering in the United Kingdom. In the words of Steve Jobs, co-founder of

Apple, Inc., "We're here to put a dent in the universe," which was exactly what she did.

Ultimately, the overlap of Darego's win and Adichie's speech gave me the drive to find my own voice, one that was borderless and went beyond my national identity as a Nigerian. I realized that if these Nigerian women could move the world so profoundly, I could too.

Soon after, CNN announced its new tagline: "Go Beyond Borders". It was the last push I needed. I was now on a quest to find my voice. Once I realized it was possible to go beyond borders to make an impact, I took a leap of faith and did it. I found my borderless voice.

WHY THIS BOOK?

This book is about finding your borderless voice. It shows you how to transcend your limitations and make a valuable contribution to the world. You are not a product of your environment, but of your own design, vision, and voice. It doesn't matter where you come from. Your story might be confined to a geographical location, but your voice doesn't need to be. It can have an impact on the world. The environment that has shaped your story and worldview is your greatest asset and advantage.

This book is about self-empowerment. It echoes the fact that borders are not just physical, but mental. Those who move across international borders must do so also in the mind. The greatest border is your own self-perception; it's a case of mistaken identity. Such an identity crisis permeates every facet of life, be it personal, professional or cultural. On a larger scale, it is not only a national problem but a global one as well.

These chapters provide the toolkit one needs to go beyond the mental boundaries that may entrap you. They will help you to retain a healthy and strong sense of identity. This book is for those who called a new country home. For those who feel invisible, helpless, or are treated as if they are "foreign". It is for those who identify as a minority and feel disadvantaged. This book provides a means to reclaim your power. It will inspire new perspectives.

Otherness doesn't have to be a weakness. It can be—in fact, it is—one's greatest asset.

I have had opportunities to live, work, and invest in different countries, which has established me as a business leader and allowed me to help countless individuals. In these pages, I share my journey and the defining moments that shaped my distinct story. I will also include the stories of many individuals I have successfully coached as an Identity Strategist.

Find your borderless voice.

Tell your story.

Define your identity.

PART I

IDENTITY

CHAPTER ONE

The International Entrepreneur

There is no passion to be
found in playing small – in settling
for a life that is less than the one you
are capable of living.

—*Nelson Mandela*

I DIDN'T WAKE UP on October 24, 2014 planning to change my life so dramatically. It just happened. Looking back, I am reminded how quickly our lives can change when we begin to see ourselves, our career path, and our paradigms differently, even if that difference is very small. For me, and others I've worked with, the defining moments of our lives are often clothed with what appears to be a mundane event, yet that simple event often alters our world.

I was at the Hartsfield-Jackson International Airport, flying from Lagos, Nigeria, en route to New York. There, I was attending a conference, but I also had the intention of doing business in the United States. At the point of entry into the U.S., the immigration officer requested to see my Nigerian passport. "What is your purpose in the United States?" he asked.

As a frequent visitor to the U.S., I considered my response. The two options set before me were either "immigrant" or "visitor." Neither of these labels best defined or resonated with me any longer. Culturally, I identified as being African. Spiritually, I was Christian. My national identity was as a Nigerian, however, I had lived and worked as an expat in Washington, D.C. for more than a year.

"What is your mission in the United

States?" the immigration officer repeated. "What do you do?" It was, I realized, a defining moment. Rather than acquiesce to labels that did not capture the true essence of who I am, and who I was becoming as an international entrepreneur, I decided to define who I was in terms of my international identity. To do so was risky. According to U.S. immigration law, an individual can only be admitted back into the country as a returning citizen, resident, or visitor.

"I am an entrepreneur," I replied. "I'm back in the States to start a new business."

"What?" He exclaimed. "How can you run a business in the U.S. without being a U.S. citizen or permanent resident? I'm sorry but I can't authorize your entry. I have to refer you to secondary screening."

An officer escorted me to an interview room. I wasn't alone. There was a male of middle eastern descent, a West African nursing mother, and a Latino family. As we awaited our fates, I felt the flux of varying emotions. Had I made the right choice? I could have told them I was here for a conference or that I was visiting family or a business partner.

It would only have delayed the inevitable, I thought, attempting to reassure myself.

My luggage was pulled from the plane to New York. The flight was temporarily delayed, but for how long? I watched as, one by one, the others around me were denied entry. Their hopes and dreams were dashed. They would not see the land of opportunity.

Our identities were being defined, I realized. As was our fate.

"Gbenga Ogunjimi," I heard over the intercom. It was the clearest pronunciation I had ever heard from a non-Yoruba speaker. Every syllable of my Nigerian name was carefully articulated over the loudspeaker. My verdict had been reached.

With my carry-on luggage, I proceeded to the immigration agent. My heart raced. I thought of all the possibilities—what could be or could have been. I braced myself for the worst while hoping for the best, all the while wondering if I could have been more convincing. What I found daunting was the notion that immigrants were leeches on the American system. The term "immigrants" had come to be synonymous with individuals seeking economic refuge.

I was no leech. For the past two years, I had dedicated my career to serve the country as an international exchange visitor in Washington D.C. Not only was I an international business owner, I employed Americans. And, I paid taxes.

"We have reached a decision on your case," the officer stated. "We decided to let you into the United States, again."

I sighed, relieved. The anticipation and anxiety I felt gave way to elation.

"Yes, we can tell you run a business," he explained, "but we will have you change to a permanent status, and this is how to go about it...."

My new international identity had been created!

I now had something that many foreigners and immigrants did not: The power to define myself. I chose to shift my paradigm of who I was, and identify myself with a borderless, international identity.

I am an International Entrepreneur, living in the United States!

What had changed? I was the same as I had always been, but my paradigm had shifted. In the brief time, it took to change my answer to an immigration officer, I had changed my image of myself for me, and for him. I would continue to change others with that one simple thing—a paradigm shift.

CHAPTER TWO

Paradigm

*All the significant breakthroughs were
breaks "withs" old ways of thinking*

—*Thomas Kuhn*

WHAT IS A PARADIGM? I ask this question because to tell your story, unleash your "borderless voice," get past the stuck or confused place in your life, you must undergo a paradigm shift. First of all, a paradigm is neither good nor bad. It is simply how you see the world. Your paradigms are a set of concepts, practices or thought patterns that create a framework we use to define our way of looking at something. Later in this book, you will see how the people I worked with confronted the way they thought about themselves, and learned to retell their story to seize on their potential and their best self.

For instance, if you encounter a person speeding and weaving dangerously through traffic, how do you feel? What do you think? Do you get angry, frightened, or annoyed? What if you learned that the driver is trying to get their injured or dying child to the hospital? Does your paradigm (thoughts about the event) change? If your boss or co-worker is angry and short-tempered with you, do you feel resentful? What if you learned they were going through a divorce or a serious health crisis? Would your attitude (paradigm) change?

It's amazing how our attitudes, thoughts, and expectations adjust immediately when new information, knowledge, or experiences provide us with a new found understanding.

Not only does our paradigm shift, but everything from our feelings, our attitude, and even our physical state-of-being shifts! As you see, the paradigm is a powerful tool. Ask yourself "what are my paradigms? How do I view the world? Is that view helpful or harmful to me?" Now, consider how a shift in your existing paradigms can benefit you.

A paradigm shift is a gradual change in which your framework of thoughts and concepts are gradually replaced by new thoughts and concepts. Because how we see the world is filtered through our paradigms, we project our thought patterns onto others based on our own personal history and experiences. If a person you are in communication with has a different paradigm than the one you have, things can get very volatile, very quickly! Likewise, if someone shares our paradigm, we can bond very quickly.

Many things define our paradigms – our culture, our family, our nationality, our upbringing, our religion, our politics, our social structure, our age, gender, and education. But the same things that define our paradigms, can also change them.

For instance, our age defines our paradigms. The life of a child is different than the life of an adult. It is the aging and the change from a dependent to a worker that creates the paradigm shift. When a teenager who has never worked becomes an employee, their paradigms around what it means to be an income producer versus a dependent, shifts. As your paradigms shift, so does your identity: the way you see yourself, your way of life, your goals, what matters, and what doesn't matter to you. The right paradigm shift can break you, paralyze or empower you. So, while many things in your life may change, a paradigm shift recreates you. When I made the decision to see myself as an international entrepreneur, the way I thought about myself, my future, my business, and the people around me changed dramatically. It was risky for me, but once I made the shift and claimed my voice I had a new story to tell. It was a story that would be so much more powerful than the one I had been telling.

Something deeply significant happens when the usual way of thinking about or doing something is replaced by a new and different way, and that is why a paradigm shift in an individual is the prelude to a paradigm shift in society, and then ultimately, the world. Learning to become aware of your existing paradigms, and to notice when they shift, is not only empowering, it's how visionaries and leaders are born. This is the foundation for a borderless, unstoppable, uncontrollable and invincible voice.

PARADIGM SHIFTS

The 20th century showed us that nothing is set in stone. There have been more monumental paradigm shifts in the last 100–150 years than in all of recorded history. From the paradigm shifts in religion – Martin Luther may be considered the most obvious religious paradigm shift when he nailed his ninety-five theses to the Wittenberg University church door, but that was only the tipping point of the shift. Europe was undergoing cultural, social, and political paradigm shifts long before Luther even entered the priesthood. The paradigm shift was taking place, but it was so gradual that most people did not notice. This is how most large shifts happen — in increments. They also happen with or without design, some-times simply because of other shifts people see going on around them:

The United States, contrary to what many believe, did not lead the race into space. The Soviet Union did. On Friday, October 4, 1957, the Soviets had orbited the world's first arti-ficial satellite, blazing across the night skies in a low earth orbit. The first satellite was nothing like the ones we see today. It was a very simple metal sphere the size of a beach ball. To amateur astronomers on earth, it's passing over America was visible with their home telescopes. The satellite also had four external radio antennas to broadcast radio pulses. So, its radio signal was easily detectable even by radio amateurs. The satellite weighed only 184 pounds and took only 98 minutes to orbit the Earth. Yet, that single launch ushered in one of the greatest political, military, technological, and scientific paradigm shifts in history. America got serious about space exploration when that happened. The 19th and 20th centuries were the centuries of shattering paradigms.

Then, in 1968, two overlapping events occurred that changed America forever. The first was the assassination of Dr. Martin Luther King, Jr., which was the tipping point of the civil rights movement. It marked the end of a Jim Crow segregated south.

The second was the Apollo 8 mission, the first manned spacecraft to successfully leave Earth's orbit and reach the Moon. What's more, it then orbited the Moon and returned safely to Earth. Man had conquered what had previously been considered impossible—and made it possible.

Both of these events were monumental paradigm shifts that came about because of shifts that happened before them. Both proved that concrete borders weren't so "set" after all. The implications of these shifts have continued to unfold, even to this present day. But the shifts didn't happen overnight, or with that one historically significant event.

The paradigm of what it meant to be black in America, or what it would take to leave the confines of earth and travel into outer space had been building over the decades. When Rosa Parks refused to sit at the back of the bus, when groups of black men and women staged sit-ins at lunch counters, when schools became integrated – all these were small paradigm shifts that would ultimately lead to King's assassination and the civil rights movement that followed. There were other events that altered America's progress as a nation.

There are dozens, if not hundreds of other records, other paradigms that have been changed over the centuries. The one thing they all have in common is that they didn't happen in a vacuum. In other words, each paradigm shifted after a culmination of concepts, practices, and ideas had begun to shift, paving the way for the framework to change. While running or flying seconds faster than another human being or climbing a mountain no one had ever scaled before may seem small given the world's more pressing problems, what matters is that they prove paradigm shifts in our thoughts. These are what result in real lasting changes in behavior and mindset because they achieve seemingly impossible feats. We rarely know at the moment it occurs what will come of our shift. In fact, it may take decades for the world to see the change, but they a person shifts their understanding of themselves or the world, they will sense that internal change immediately.

Einstein said, *"We can not solve our problems with the same level of thinking that created them."*

What he meant was that true change must come from a personal paradigm shift, not from a conventional problem-solving mode. Trying to figure out how to fix things, especially if thinking your way through a problem has failed in the past, won't work. You must experience a paradigm shift, an alteration of your unconscious. It's amazing how many problems evaporate right in front of your eyes once your paradigm changes.

Before you embark on a paradigm shift understand first that a paradigm is a mental setting. They are deeply embedded in our psyche. You can't just flip a switch, read a book, or chant positive affirmations – although those strategies can help. There isn't a clear-cut way to access or alter our paradigms. The context inside your mind where you think, feel and live must change for you to experience a shift.

Tips and tricks, improving your personal discipline, none of that will work until you understand what your subconscious mind truly wants.

Your paradigm literally determines what you hold onto, mentally and emotionally. Have you ever felt you had a problem you wanted to let go of, but couldn't figure out exactly how to let go? You're not alone. Most of us are holding onto problems we can't figure out how to escape. We hang onto the problem because somewhere, deep inside, we believe (consciously or not) that our survival depends on the set of beliefs and the framework we follow. When we undergo a paradigm shift, our tendency to hold onto these thoughts and feelings completely transforms.

You can't create a new strategy to fix a long-lasting problem without having a paradigm shift first. Even if you find a solution, you will only revert, time and time again, to the same old problems and keep wondering why permanent change continues to elude you.

Paradigm shifts require several things:

- You must understand what your current

paradigm is and how you see the world now. Remember that a paradigm is a multitude of habits that are lodged in your subconscious mind. Paradigms are the assumptions we hold about the way the world is. Paradigms are the reality we create and then project upon the world. Understanding how you see the world is critical to understanding how to change that assumption. Spend 10 minutes on any social media site and it's easy to see that people definitely see the world differently!

- Paradigm shifts require that you understand that paradigms are deeper than attitudes or behaviors. They are deeply held *beliefs* about the way life is or should be. Any discussion involving politics, homelessness, religion, abortion, or money management – any hot-button topic – will quickly reveal a person's deepest paradigms!

- To shift from your current paradigm to a new one, you must deliberately create a different paradigm by exposing yourself to the paradigms of others as well as to the new paradigms you want to embrace.

- You must consciously change your paradigms in the same way they were created—through repetition of information – in this case, new information.

- You must understand that to change a paradigm you have to consciously and deliberately replace a "bad" habit with a "good" habit, or one thought/belief with another. Otherwise, you're going to form another bad habit because nature abhors a vacuum.

- Finally, start the process by consciously choosing new beliefs that are aligned with the habits and life you want, and then plant them in the place of the old beliefs in your subconscious mind. Water the new habits and beliefs daily – mindfully correcting the old thoughts and beliefs with the new when you see them arise.

· Now you can begin to develop your "borderless voice".

CHAPTER THREE

What is a Borderless Voice?

All the forces in the world are not so
powerful as an idea whose time has come.

—*Victor Hugo*

LET'S BEGIN WITH WHAT your voice is. In literature, a "voice" is the form or a format through which the narrator tells their story. A strong voice comes across when a writer can place their personality into the story. The reader gets, feels that the character is a real person, and is conveying a specific message the writer wants to communicate. To put it simply, a book's "voice" is an author's unique writing style or point of view. In life, your voice is your brand. It's who you are, what you stand for, who you are outside of what you do.

When you find your voice, you have found your purpose, and that purpose has become the story you are now living to tell. A "Borderless Voice" happens when these manifestations become completely unencumbered by any barriers, beliefs, or old paradigms. My voice was "International entrepreneur." As you'll see later in the book, different people find their voice when they find themselves — their story, their purpose, their calling. You will too.

So, this is what a borderless voice looks like; the moment you connect to an overarching purpose for life and make a meaningful contribution to the world you reach a point of transcendence where you become unstoppable by the external perceptions of your identity. This voice is the intersection of your life's purpose, story, and identity

— your voice. When you combine that voice with a paradigm shift, that is when you begin to change your world, and that is when you begin to change *the* world.

Throughout the rest of this book, I'll share stories about ordinary people who by choosing to tell their stories, and by creating a paradigm shift, became extraordinary catalysts for change in their communities. The strategies I share will make it possible for you to find your borderless voice and expand your impact in the world. American television and radio personality Peter Marshall once said, "the measure of life is not its duration but its donation." This is what finding your voice, and shifting your limiting paradigms, is all about. The moment you start living the truest and most authentic version of your life, you will inspire everyone around you to do the same.

HAVE YOU IDENTIFIED YOUR BORDERS AND EXAMINED YOUR LIMITING PARADIGMS?

Finding one's borderless voice starts with identifying one's borders and paradigms about yourself on the mental, physical, spiritual, intellectual and relational level:

Borders are not just physical, they are mental. I am talking about those self-limiting mindsets and paradigms that can propel you forward or hold you back. To go beyond mental borders, ask yourself, does your life's vision transcend your present geographical location? Do you have a written life plan that reaches beyond years, decades, and possibly the next generation? The borders that limit you are your current paradigms. When you change your limits, you change your borders.

Borders are not just mental; they are intellectual. Here I'm talking about the necessary skill-sets that could accelerate or impede your competitiveness in the global world. To overcome intellectual borders, ask yourself if your personal brand leverages technology and social media platforms to monetize your talents. Does it maximize the impact you are seeking to create in the world? What are your paradigms around your intellectual skills, or your perceived lack of them?

Borders are not just intellectual; they are artificial. These are self-imposed barriers you impose on your own personal growth and professional advancements. Ask yourself, what disempowering mindsets have you brought to your life challenges? By this, I mean what are the negative beliefs— "I can't", "Not for me" or "Us vs. Them" or "I'm not smart enough, qualified, or experienced enough," that you've accepted as a part of your vocabulary?

Borders are not just artificial; they are relational. I am referring here to those people in your primary circle of influence and the role they play. Is your circle comprised of supportive mentors, coaches, accountability partners, promoters, and cheerleaders? This network should have the capacity and resources to support your life's vision and goals.

Borders are not just relational; they are spiritual – Have you considered what your spiritual borders are? By this, I am talking about the daily routines and spiritual practices that could strengthen or undermine who you are and how authentically you lead your life. What values do you live by and how are these values a cardinal part of your work and life choices?

In the next chapters of this book, I will be speaking more in detail about these borders. I will share stories of how ordinary people became extraordinary leaders by recognizing and overcoming their limiting boundaries. By overcoming them, they each unleashed their own, unique borderless voices, and by their own volition, transformed their identity and brand. You can, too.

GOING THROUGH THE BORDER

Overcoming your border barriers have everything to do with your paradigm. This is your mindset, perceptions, and worldview. According to Stephen Covey, the author of *7 Habits of Highly Effective People*, "If you want to make minor, incremental changes and improvements, work on practices, behavior or attitude. But if you want to make significant, quantum improvements, work on the paradigm."

What's your paradigm as far as your international identity is concerned?

Regardless of nationality, ethnicity or race, understand the value of who you are. This is your brand identity. Your value is first and foremost as an individual. It's not where you come from or where you're going. In order to establish your international identity, you must relinquish these three paradigms:

1. Immigrant paradigm – You are not an immigrant, you are international.

As British-American writer Taiye Selasi puts it in her famous TED Talk, "Don't ask me where I'm from, ask me where I'm a local", "As an immigrant knows, the question where are you from, or where you are really from, is often code for why are you here?" Identifying as an immigrant in a borderless world has nothing to do with nationality or residency, it is a state of mind. It is most empowering to see yourself as an international, skilled professional; an investor, entrepreneur, and so on. When you define yourself as a citizen of one country, you cut yourself off from being a citizen of the world.

2. Minority paradigm – You may be *in the minority* in a group, or a culture, or a country, but you are not a minority—you are a brand. Your brand is your promise to the world around you. As *Entrepreneur Magazine* puts it, "It tells your customers what they can expect from your products and services, and it differentiates your offering from your competitors'. Your brand is derived from who you are, who you want to be and who people perceive you to be." Norwegian playwright and poet, Henrik Ibsen once said: "The majority is always wrong; the minority is rarely right." It doesn't matter if you are demographically classified as a minority, whether you are Black, Latino or Asian, see it as an asset, not a disadvantage because you possess perspectives that are unique to your experience. Within these specificities lie your value as an individual and your brand identity.

3. **Environment paradigm** – You don't have to become a product of your environment. You have a story to tell. You can create yourself into someone of your own design, vision, and voice, or be a victim to your environment. TED Global speaker Becky Blanton, speaking about her 18 months of homelessness, tells people, "Homelessness is not who you are. It's *where* you are. Who

you are is different from what is happening to you, or around you at any given moment." While your story might be confined to a geographical location or a space in time, your voice doesn't need to be. It can be borderless and make an impact on this world.

CHAPTER FOUR

Your Brand Identity

All of us need to understand the importance of branding. We are CEOs of our own companies: Me, Inc. To be in business today, our most important job is to be head marketer for the brand called You.

– Tom Peters

DEFINING YOUR BRAND IDENTITY

TO DEFINE YOUR BRAND identity, let's first define what is a brand is and what it is not.

Your brand identity is not your website, social media or the services you are known for; those help shape your brand, but they are secondary. First and foremost, you are the brand. From your name to your personality. The goal here is to take a panoramic view of the various aspects of your life to examine what your brand is.

A brand is your identity, it tells the world what they can expect from you, what you will deliver, how they will feel doing business with you, and why you are a better choice than your competition. Do not take this process of developing your brand lightly. It is what you will build the rest of your business and career on, and it is how you will come to be known in the world.

To simplify this, a brand is what identifies you to your customers. A brand delivers a message that:

- **Confirms your credibility.** It tells people you are reliable, trustworthy, competent, and honest in your dealings.

- **Emotionally connects your target audience with your product and or service.** People do business with people they like and trust. People will come to you because you and your brand, make them feel good about themselves and about doing business with you.

- **Motivates the buyer to buy.** People buy because they trust the product and the business owner who stands behind it. When people trust your brand, they feel safe doing business with you and will refer their friends to you.

- **Creates User Loyalty.** Human beings are predictable in that we stick to people, places, products and businesses we feel comfortable with, and with whom we've been satisfied with in the past. When your brand demonstrates you can be consistently trusted to deliver good services or products over time, you automatically create user loyalty.

We'll explore this from a personal, professional, relational, entrepreneurial, physical, spiritual, social, and international perspective. This vision should stretch to a year, but ideally be a decade long. Why this timeline? A long-term perspective is important as a core discipline for finding your borderless voice and for telling a story that manifests your life's goals.

YOUR BRAND IDENTITY VISION

Creating a 360-degree vision for your brand identity is no doubt one of the most exciting and excruciating exercises. This singular discipline is a core distinction between doers and dreamers; between those who only talk about their aspiration and those who manifest theirs repeatedly. It separates leaders from followers; visionaries and those without a vision. It distinguishes creators and consumers; those that create and monetize their contents, and those that only consumes the contents others create.

To create this brand identity plan, let's' explore these principles:

1. **Start with an overview effect –** Otherwise known as the big picture perspective, this strategy comes from the first manned space exploration I mentioned earlier. An overview effect happens when you have a panoramic

perspective of your brand. To practice or acquire an overview perspective, you must understand that you are not what you do. *What you do is an expression of who you are.*

2. **Practice intentional congruence** – This is the process of aligning your ideas, efforts, and resources so they are in harmony with each other. Intentional congruence is also applied in the industry of financial investments; when you bring your multiple streams of income into a single business entity. The application of this to your 360-brand identity vision, is being able to interlace the various facets of your brand i.e. personal, family, career etc.

3. **Practice Idealization** – This is an imaginary state of perfection. To practice idealization, think about this: if resources, opportunities, skills, connections were not a barrier, what would

the life you want to lead look like? How would you want to live, where would you want to be, and what do you see yourself accomplishing in your lifetime? What's your work-life balance vision?

4. **Practice reverse engineering** – Now that you have this vision, capture it on a vision board, and reverse engineer the process – meaning you work backwards. Start at the end and work back to the beginning to see what it would take for you to arrive at your goal. For example, if you envision a career that allows you to put your passion to work and spending more time with your family is your end goal. Now, ask yourself, with this goal, what must I do to achieve it? You might find that dedicating a set amount of time with your family over working more hours is helpful. You might find that you need to create a work schedule that either allows you

to work from home or one that ensures you are available to be with your family during consistent hours in the evening. That might require a shift in responsibilities, hiring additional people, delegating more tasks. Once you know what you want, then it will be easier to determine what you need to do to reach that goal.

If you want to be a doctor, then you reverse engineer that and see that you will have to attend college, complete your residency, and an internship and pay for school. Paying for school might mean delaying gratification of buying a new car or a house so that you can afford your tuition. Reverse engineering our goals is a way of "counting the costs" of what our dream or vision will demand from us. Some people will decide, after this exercise, that maybe their goal is too big, or not big enough.

CHAPTER FIVE

360 Identity Overview

*Too many people overvalue what they
are not and undervalue what they are.*

—Malcolm Forbes

NOW LET'S EXPLORE the eight components
of your brand identity and how do define your
identity in each category:

1. Personal Identity

2. Professional Identity

3. Family Identity

4. Health Identity

5. Financial Identity

6. Spiritual Identity

7. Community Identity

8. Tribe Identity

PERSONAL IDENTITY

I. Personal Identity—If you are you are no longer identified being as a parent, worker, business owner etc. What ONE word most resonates with who you are?

II. Survival Skills and Talent—What is the one skill you could depend on to support you outside of your current means of income?

III. Passion and Drives—What would you describe to be your passion in its purest form. What are you motivated by—the need to serve, make a profit or to make your voice heard?

IV. Personal Core Values—What are you core guiding principles and beliefs?

V. Personal Mission Statement— In one sentence, what is your personal mission statement?

PROFESSIONAL IDENTITY

I. Professional Identity – It important to preface this category by saying regardless of your professional level at this point *you are a leader*. It doesn't matter if you are entry, mid, senior or management – you are a leader. With this in mind, ending with the word "leader" to your current industry, how would you define yourself professional wise – business leader, nonprofit leader etc.

II. Vision for Success —What is your vision for highest professional aspiration at this time?

III. Educational Goals—What formal education or training would help you to accomplish this aspiration.

IV. Learning Goals—What informal education or training would help you to accomplish this aspiration.

V. Mentors and Professional coaches—Have you identified and recruited the mentors and coaches that have the capacity to help you get to this aspiration.

VI. Statement —What is your professional mission statement.

Family Identity

I. Family identity—This speaks to the ideals you want your family to be known for and principles which you collectively chose to be governed by. The goal here is to have a generational perspective; a continuation of your family story, vision, and legacy. These ideals started before you and should go on to the next generation. With this in mind, think about the identity do you want your family to be known for.

II. Family heritage—Think about your heritage this way, from both of your parents y; going back to two or three generations— What commonalities do you have with them? Meaning, what are the distinct traits or attributes you share with them?

III. Family Legacy—What vision is your family trying to create or perpetuate for the coming generation?

IV. Family Mission Statement—In one sentence, define your family's mission statement.

Financial Identity

I. Financial Freedom—I am looking at financial freedom from the perspective of monetizing your talents. The survival skills and talents we covered in the personal identity component is the foundation for this. It helps you create an economic machinery for your brand and achieve financial freedom.

II. Wealth—What is your getting into wealth plan through the creation of multiple streams of income?

III. Debt—What is your plan for getting out of debt?

IV. Investment—What is your investment

plan, be it real estate, money markets or angel investments?

V. Giving—The act of giving is both altruistic and strategic. It is strategic in it allows you to direct your financial resources after paying your taxes to the causes that important to you. It is altruistic in that it is the generous and right thing to do.

VI. Retirement—I do not mean retirement in the traditional sense of using the time after working life for relaxation and hobbies. Rather, what is the expected timeline of making the ultimate transition from your day job to your purpose and calling. Your purpose and life's assignment are the greatest conduits to your financial freedom and wealth.

VII. Statement— In one sentence, what is your financial mission statement?

Tribe Identity

I. Now that you can see yourself as a brand, this perspective must be reflected in your community and power network. Many mistake the word power network for a support network, although they sound very similar, they are not the name. A support network is a sub-component of a power network and these are what the power network consists of.

II. Personal Board of Directors—Do you have a personal board of director that can help bring your life's aspiration to life? How professionally and culturally diverse is this group?

III. Inner Circle—Who are the five closest people to you and what role do they play in your life right now?

IV. Support Network—Do you have an emotional support community? Does this community consist of mentors, coaches, doctors, investors and accountability partners?

V. Alliances & Strategic Partners—Does your brand collaborate with corporate organizations that provide platforms to monetize your story and talents?

VI. Statement— In one sentence, what is your tribe statement?

Spiritual Identity

I. Spiritual Identity—Your spiritual identity is not about your religion or faith, although that might play a role in it. Spiritual identity speaks to your core beliefs and values. It is important because it makes your personal brand authentic and grounded in your values. The goal here is to be able to develop spiritual competency and have mastery of your spiritual intelligence. How do you identify spiritually?

II. Routine—What are your daily spiritual routine and practices?

III. Advisor—Do you have a spiritual mentor, coach or advisor?

IV. Tribe—Have you identified a community that is compatible with your core beliefs and cores? Does this community help your gifts to mature and flourish?

V. Values—What are your core spiritual values and beliefs and where do they come from? Were you raised with them? Do you believe in them strongly, or just follow them because you were raised that way? Are they a true part of who you are at your core? How easily (if at all) can they be shaken or compromised?

VI. Statement— In one sentence, what is your spiritual mission statement?

Health Identity

I. Nutrition—The quality of your health as a direct correlation to every aspect of your life.

II. Mental Health— – How are you planning to improve your mental health? This is self-growth and awareness. It's about bettering yourself as a person.

III. Exercise—Do you have an exercise routine you are committed to?

IV. Sleeping—Sleep is very undervalued in our culture. How do you plan to maintain a healthy sleeping cycle?

V. Reading—The average person reads less

than 15 books a year. How many books to plan to read every year?

VI. Detox—Do you practice physical, dietary, emotional, or spiritual detox as part of a way of staying healthy?

VII. Statement— In one sentence or two, what is your health and wellness statement?

Community & International Identity

I. International Identity—I spoke earlier the process of establishing my own international identity, an aspect I had previously accepted and not defined. What is your identity? How do you see yourself outside of your home country?

II. Community—What is your leadership role in your community?

III. Foundation—Have your considered

starting a personal or foundation to deepen your impact in your community

IV. Service—Do you have a local and international you volunteer and donate to?

V. Statement— In one sentence or two, what is your community and international identity statement?

PART II
STORY

CHAPTER SIX

The Fashion Psychologist

Many stories matter. Stories have been used to dispose and to malign, but stories can also be used to empower and to humanize. Stories can break the dignity of a people, but stories can also repair that broken dignity.

—Chimamanda Ngozi Adichie

CAPE VERDE IS Africa's best-kept secret. It's a paradise island known for its artistic culture, diversity, and captivating beauty. It was from this country that Sandra's family came to America in the late 1800s to join the bolster-ing Cape Verdean community of New England. Like many immigrants, entrepreneurship was their way of survival. They told their own story, the version they believed embodied their truth and cultural tradition. They chose the sewing trade: fashion. As with any enterprise, business fluctuated. Some days were high, others low. Particularly for this Cape Verdean family, there was the immigrant stigma – the identity of being defined not by who you were, but by what you did.

However, despite the fact that Sandra was born into a tradition of fashion entrepre-neurs, she was determined to escape the family mold and carve her own path. Unlike her predecessors, she pursued a degree in psychology and her career blossomed. She rose to become a social case manager for the YMCA, then later at the Massachusetts Department of Transitional Assistance. Unbeknownst to her, a bigger plan lay in wait for her. Despite her chosen path, wherever she went, people complimented her iconic sense of style. Sandra was that black woman at the job interview who got away with having silver, blue or purple hair.

Successful as she was, her course as a psychologist was not enough to satisfy her yearning for purpose. She wanted her career to fulfill a sense of calling. If only she could pinpoint what it was. Sandra decided to leave the security of her job in Boston, and in a leap of faith, she moved to Washington DC. It was there, that our paths crossed.

As an Identity Strategist, I work with leaders like Sandra, who are in transition. I help them to architect their brand identity and tell their story. Sandra hired me to coach her through this journey. After a series of coaching sessions, she made a major breakthrough. We had been working on defining her mission. Sandra sent me this: "The Fashion Psychologist." Her mission was to help women match how they see themselves in their minds with how they present themselves with their wardrobe.

With her help, women began to see that

what one wears externally truly reflects who they are within, allowing them to actualize their potential and feel more confident about themselves. Sandra found the union between her training and calling, and her true self.

Sandra married her professional training with her personal interests and cultural influences to create a business that was uniquely tailored to her strengths. Since then, she has established herself as an expert in the niche of fashion psychology. She created a community of women of all ages who embrace self-expression through their wardrobes. Sandra then launched her personal brand: Sandra Marie. She also started a style-coaching business, SENDIII, and two workshop series called Holistic Fashionistas and Sweat the Runway.

Focus on the Things You Can Control

Sandra, The Fashion Psychologist, is living proof that while we do not have control over external factors such as family heritage, we do get to choose our story, rather than our story choosing us. The sooner we embrace this truth, the quicker we permit our genius to come alive, and our lights to shine.

Rather than embrace this possibility, however, too many people live by a predetermined narrative that doesn't corroborate the inner, true version of themselves. In so doing, they fail to grasp that unhelpful narrations hang like dead weight around their necks. Only by letting them go can they find the most authentic version of themselves and their story.

CHAPTER SEVEN

Telling Your Story

Those who tell the stories, rule the world.

—*A Native American Proverb*

YOUR STORY IS NOT *just* your past-to-date, instead, it's your proximity to your dreams. True storytelling is an act of co-creation and an opportunity to bring your aspirations within your reach. To do this, here are eight distinctions of between the story that manifests your dreams, and the ones that do not.

DISTINCTION 1 – Scarcity versus Abundance.

DISTINCTION 2 – Dark versus Light.

DISTINCTION 3 – Past versus Dreams.

DISTINCTION 4 – Needs versus Vision.

DISTINCTION 5 – Head versus Spirit.

DISTINCTION 6 – Follower versus Leader.

DISTINCTION 7 – Consumer versus Creator.

DISTINCTION 8 – Victim versus Overcomer.

The Distinctions

DISTINCTION 1—Scarcity versus Abundance – Like begets like. People with a scarcity paradigm will rarely tell a story that will inspire collaboration or one that will co-create opportunities. Scarcity in storytelling is something that many do unconsciously until one's attention is drawn to it. In my experience with story coaching, I've found that the number one reason people do not tell their story is that they think that their story is not important or audience-worthy. Abundance starts with the recognition that you're unique, and that no one in the world has your story. In fact, your story is the missing piece the world is waiting for, and it's the conduit for co-creating abundance for you and your audience or tribe.

DISTINCTION 2—Dark versus Light – When you tell your story, do not leave your audience in the dark. Bring them to the light. While the challenging and dark episodes of your narrative might be able to elicit an emotional response, they don't often inspire your intended outcome or a buy-in from the audience. They generate pity, not inspiration. Therefore, ensure that your story is one that leads your audience to the place of inspiration, and not a gloomy recounting of a litany of mishaps, misfortunes, and tragedies.

DISTINCTION 3—Past versus Dreams – Tell your story from a forward-looking, inspirational, and aspirational perspective. This is because any opportunity to introduce yourself or opportunity to tell your story is an opportunity to manifest your dreams. Your audience becomes your tribe, waiting for you to create these dreams together with them. Therefore, do not waste this moment on just recounting past, especially on events that have no correlation to your dreams.

DISTINCTION 4—Needs versus Vision – Whether you are pitching for an investment, fundraising for a cause, or interviewing for your job, as harsh as it might sound, understand this, your needs do not inspire others. Start with a vision instead. When you tell your story by sharing a clear vision, you will be amazed to see how quickly the distance from your reality to your aspiration collapses. However, it is your vision that makes this happen, not your needs. Remember, needs are a turn-off, it is a vision that inspires.

DISTINCTION 5—Head versus Spirit – Your heart is the seat of your emotions. When you speak from your head (mind), you reach the head (mind) but when you come from the spirit you touch your audience at their heart. Remember a time when you had a prepared speech or a script for a conversation but you decided to follow your guts and speak from your heart instead? This is what *coming from the spirit* is; it is allowing yourself to be emotional and even vulnerable when telling your story. As Brene Brown says – "Vulnerability is the birthplace of innovation, creativity, and change. Courage starts with showing up and letting ourselves be seen. Vulnerability sounds like truth and feels like courage. Truth and courage aren't always comfortable, but they're never weakness."

DISTINCTION 6—Follower versus Leader— When you tell your story as a leader, you manifest leadership opportunities. "Leadership is not a position or a title, it is action and example" says Cory Booker. Regardless of your title, whether entry, mid, senior or management level, tell your story as a leader. Understand the position doesn't make a leader, it only allows you to manifest your leadership. This distinction makes all the difference when telling your story. Later in this book, I will share the stories of ordinary people, who by telling their story as leaders became extraordinary catalysts for change in their communities. So, tell your story as a leader.

DISTINCTION 7—Consumer versus Creator—Yes, everyone as a story to tell. And when you tell your story, come from a place of creation. By *creation* I mean, create content, value, support, opportunities and so on. This is one of the profound skills I learned from a mentor of mine, Melissa G Wilson. She calls it *Supporting Your Current Efforts*. I have seen this open unimaginable door of opportunities around the world. When telling your story, identify something of value you can support your audience even if it is something as simple as an emotional or informational support. When you do this, you become a *creator* of transformational opportunities.

DISTINCTION 8—Victim versus Overcomer – You are not a victim of your circumstance, you are a survivor, a hero, an overcomer. If your goal is it elicit an emotional support, then you can tell your story as a victim. But if you intend to be the captain of your destiny and change your negative circumstances to one that is positive and empowering, then you will have to identify as an overcomer. I will be elaborating on how to this in the section *changing the narrative* and the chapter *moments.*

The Power of Your Story

Storytelling is your strongest asset. "Those who tell stories, rule the world," said Plato. Stories are like fingerprints. You are the only one with your story, not just in your hometown or city, but in the world. The uniqueness of your story is valuable in that if properly told it allows you to stand out from your competition. It doesn't matter if you are trying to secure a job, raise capital, or pursue a market share opportunity. Starting with your story is an incredible way to connect with a potential employer, venture capitalist, or potential partner because, while it is unique, it is likely to touch on meaningful, universal themes. Such moments often resonate with others, helping you to connect. So, embrace your story.

Storytelling also activates your tribe. When you tell your story, you activate your "tribe." Your tribe is a community of like-minded individuals who share common interests and values. It is within this tribe where miracles happen. Notice, I didn't use the world create but activate. You activate your tribe. It has always been there, waiting for you to come into yourself and find your true voice. Sandra is a perfect case-in-point. Coming from a place of authenticity, she shared her story, thus activating the community that bolstered her to success.

Third, storytelling creates new opportunities. The saying "you are enough" may be a cliché, but it is without a doubt true. Your story contains latent opportunities you have yet to realize; the re-telling of it often brings hidden possibilities to light. It makes it possible to journey to your highest aspirations. Whether you want to get published, launch your own business, secure a deal, or make a significant impact in your community, it is the conduit by which to reach such goals.

Fourth, storytelling establishes your credibility. Telling your story allows you to own and monetize your accomplishments. This is important. People often don't fully own their most positive attributes. Instead, they struggle to give themselves permission. I see this in individuals in career transitions. They fail to see their strengths and cannot appreciate their unique abilities. This makes it difficult to be the architect of one's own professional identity and personal brand. The result is that they defer responsibility. Employees relinquish their power to employers and entrepreneurs to their industries. Meanwhile, only you can truly realize your potential and actualize your professional identity.

Fifth, storytelling establishes points of commonality – What unites is more than what separates. Society is bound by culture, but commonalities based on shared values, interests, vision, and experiences also serve to bond and unify. Telling your story establishes connections with others, which makes it possible to build a thriving community of supporters and power network.

Pillars of an influential story

Intentional—Whether you are interviewing for a job or pitching for capital to start a business, most times the conversation starts with some version of "can I meet you?" This is an invitation to tell your story and create a potentially long-term impression. Often times this crucial activity is left to improvisation and chance. To tell a story that activates your tribe to action, you must start with a clear intention to tell your story.

Own—The movie, *Pursuit of Happyness* starring Will Smith as Chris Gardner. In the interview scene, Chris Gardner was very determined to tell his story regardless of how unexciting or challenges-ridden it was. He was released from jail just before the interview. He had a family and personal issues, and overall his life was in a very dark place. But he made a firm decision to embrace his story without letting it define him. This approach applies to every one of us as well, we must embrace our life-defining experiences as a key aspect of our story, but also be adept in changing this narrative to achieve our intended outcome.

Authentic—Authenticity is a combination of integrity and credibility. The beauty of telling your story is that stories are inherently authentic because our story is our truth. Authentic stories come from the defining moments of our narratives. It may be good or bad, tragic or inspirational, perhaps random, or even deliberate. Your defining moment is the conduit to finding and speaking your borderless voice. Defining moments are the events of your life that have had or will have a direct effect on your life trajectory. For some, this may be a dark, painful moment like the loss of a loved one, and for others, it could be a bright, thrilling event like receiving a once-in-a-lifetime opportunity. Whichever it is, embrace these episodes of your narrative to pinpoint the most authentic version of your story

CHAPTER EIGHT

Changing the Narrative

*It is not in the stars to hold
our destiny but in ourselves.*

— Shakespeare

YOU HAVE PROBABLY HEARD the saying, "Change your narrative, change your life." Some people call it "reframing," while others call it "spinning." While "change your narrative, change your life," is true, people often think the process of changing one's narrative should happen over the course of a lifetime. This couldn't be further from the truth. Changing one's narrative occurs the moment one changes one's self-perception or paradigm. When this occurs, one's reality (and opportunities) change accordingly. It can happen in an instant, or a few minutes, or a course of days, weeks, or months. But it certainly is not required to happen over a lifetime. To explain the power of changing one's narrative—particularly a professional one—I'll share a couple of experiences with two of my coaching clients named Jane and Mike.

Jane

When I met Jane, she was in a period of professional transition. The reality of getting a job in the profession of her choice, which was highly competitive, seemed distant. After listening to her tell her story, I realized the real problem was not so much a lack of opportunities, but the way in which she told her story, not just to prospective employers, but to herself.

Compare the before and after narratives of her cover letter, especially the highlighted texts. There is a clear difference in terms of tone between the two. In the second draft of the cover letter, she finally claims her own story and professional identity. She is no longer a victim of her circumstances, but the captain of her destiny.

Jane's *before* narrative

My name is Jane D., I am seeking job opportunities in international development.

I moved from Haiti to the United States after high school in search of better opportunities. It took me two years to learn English and try to adjust to American life. When I registered for college, my parents could not support me anymore, so I took two jobs while attending classes full-time. I decided to major in Political Science because I was greatly influenced by the biographies of Nelson Mandela, Martin Luther King, and other great leaders. I wanted to learn how government functions, how decisions are made and explore strategies that work toward resolving social challenges we face today.

Upon graduating from Hunter College in New York, I decided to move to the Washington D.C. area to pursue a career in social entrepreneurship. I have applied for countless jobs in this field and attended numerous networking events, however, I have yet to receive a job offer. I tried my luck in other fields, and though I finally landed a job in banking, my passion still lies within the international realm of public policy. For this reason, I have decided to take my education to the next level by applying for a Master of Science in Global Health at Georgetown University.

Jane's *after* narrative

My name is Jane D. and I am a rising international development leader.

I came to America from Haiti to attend Hunter College in New York City. Given that my home country is non-English speaking, the adjustment to American life was somewhat challenging. I attended classes while simultaneously teaching myself English and working two jobs to fund my education.

Since childhood I have been strongly influenced by the biographies of Nelson Mandela, Martin Luther King, and other great leaders. Their life stories have ignited my calling for social justice and change, especially in developing countries like my own. I majored in political science because I wanted to learn how governments function, how decisions are made and explore strategies that work toward resolving social challenges we face globally today.

After receiving my degree, I moved to Washington D.C. to seek a career in international development, and in particular, global health. While pursuing a Master of Science in Global Health at Georgetown University, I recognized the crucial roles of business and finance within international development. For this reason, I decided to work for Capital One Financial Corporation, a bank holding company specializing in credit cards, auto loans, banking and savings products.

I am also an active volunteer at a community nonprofit expanding affordable health care in low-income communities.

Mike

When I started coaching Mike, his Asperger's syndrome was a big deal to him. In fact, he considered himself to have a disability. He felt this was something he needed to disclose for me to be comfortable and know what I was dealing with. Over time, I was able to challenge that mindset. I helped him to see that he is fine and if anything, he has an advantage most of us do not. You will see the differences in the before and after narratives below.

Mike's *before* narrative

My name is Mike K.

The last thing most people learn about me is that I have Asperger's Syndrome. I typically disclose this information after I feel like I can trust someone.

The first thing many people might observe about me is that I'm African-American.

Which is half correct. My father's family is from North Carolina, and my mother's family comes from Sierra Leone, so I view myself as both African and American.

My diagnosis and my dual heritage are the twin lenses through which I've explored and begun to work in policy. I've had to be my own advocate when school resources weren't equitably distributed.

I've collaborated with my neighbors, elected officials and Fortune 500 companies to help develop a property in my neighborhood as a commercial hub.

Most recently, my exploration of policy has taken me to Ethiopia where I worked at the African Union on crisis management and post-conflict reconstruction.

I'm applying for this fellowship program because I believe understanding the Sino-African partnership is integral to understanding the 21st Century. I believe this program would best position me to make a professional commitment to the African continent, where I hope to become a diplomat, and the U.S., where I can help communities struggling to procure resources. Thank you and I hope to see you in Beijing.

Mike's *after* narrative

I am Mike K. The two defining aspects of my identity and my path towards public service are my Asperger's syndrome and my African and American heritage.

First, I do not consider my Asperger's a disability. Great leaders like George Washington and Abraham Lincoln are considered to have had Asperger's. If anything, it makes me uniquely wired for public service. People with this diagnosis have been proven to have a natural attention to detail, be independent thinkers, and logical decision making.

Second, my father is from North Carolina and my mother is from Sierra Leone, which has greatly expanded my worldview.

I have served as a student advocate on Martin O'Malley's 2016 Presidential campaign. I have also worked tirelessly for the economic revitalization of my D.C. neighborhood and the African Union HQ in Ethiopia on post-conflict reconstruction.

It is time for me to venture out even further. I believe that China and this fellowship program are the natural steps in my trajectory toward global leadership and service.

Thank you and I hope to see you in Beijing.

CHAPTER NINE

Template for Telling Your Story

Professional Identity:
Industry leadership, professional, transitions, and aspirations.

Hero Journey:
Emotional experiences, victories, triumphs.

Defining Moments:
Aha moments, mentor, discovery, awareness.

Outcome:
Successes, results, accomplishments.

Call to action:
The ask, transferable experience, value proposition.

PART III
BRAND

CHAPTER TEN

The Spiritual Coach

*As a culture, and as individuals, we suffer
from a case of mistaken identity. This is not just
one more problem to add to our confusion – it
is the central issue.*

— Phillip Shepherd

"DRIFTING IN AND OUT of consciousness, I could faintly hear someone say, 'she is dying, she has lost so much blood, she cannot make it'."

Trapped in a vicious cycle of abusive relationships, Florence was holding on to this last relationship for her self-worth, esteem, and identity. She had been searching for love in all the wrong places and the abortions her partner demanded were her only form of birth control. She now found herself barely conscious under the anesthesia and on the operating table for her 9th procedure, the doctors fighting for her life after a botched procedure. She garnered all her remaining strength to maintain consciousness and, although still very weak, she made a life-saving decision. After so many years of family betrayals, domestic violence, homelessness, and suicide attempts, if she survived this, she was ready to do everything in her power to commit her life to something bigger than herself. She would do everything possible to be a force of change for women dealing with the same ordeal. She survived and kept her promise to herself.

The first thing she did was establish her independence as an entrepreneur. She worked for several years selling makeup through Mary Kay and was able to start the journey towards financial independence and emotional freedom. She met Dr. Patricia Bailey, a successful Christian leader who preached around the country, and started working with her as a mentee. Florence learned to refine her ability to connect, heal, and lead and quickly became more sought after in business, and in her personal life. After going back to school and obtaining a degree, she became a Minister of Faith and founded the Esther Generation Prayer Life Ministry.

Now a spiritual changemaker living in the core of her new passion and life's purpose, it was somewhat unimaginable for her to think bigger. Ministers of faith consider their work as the highest privilege and call to service any human can have. Yet Florence wrestled with an insatiable yearning to do more, give more, and touch more lives. While her desire for more was clear, what was even clearer was that being a one-woman institution was not the way for her to keep going. She realized she had to make yet another life-altering decision. She would have to aspire beyond her current professional identity as a Minister of Faith.

Florence needed a new strategy to articulate her burning desire to expand her circles of influence and impact. She wanted to stretch the impact of her transformation work beyond the walls of her ministry. Florence envisioned both a ministry without walls and being a minister without borders. She wanted to give expression to her other latent passions as an entrepreneur, philanthropist, author, speaker, and a pro-life advocate.

This is where I entered the story. Her "aha" moment happened during one of our coaching sessions. I asked her, "do you consider yourself a spiritual coach?" That was the moment she had been waiting for.

The answer to this question would unveil the next chapter of her professional life. Her initial response was, "No, I wouldn't consider myself one." However, unbeknownst to her, the very same talent, the gift of gab that enabled her freedom as an entrepreneur and activated her life's purpose as a minister of faith, was the very same talent required to make this transition as a spiritual coach.

After a series of deep coaching and self-discovery exchanges, Florence was able to give herself permission to reach beyond the labels that had defined her professional identity till that point. She made the ultimate ascension to become her own brand, a new identity that captured her many passions and talents and funneled them into a singular expression – Florence Brooks Inc.

Similar to other clients I work with to make this transition, Florence discovered she had always been enough, and that what she had been looking for was already within her reach. Her skill-set was transferrable outside of the faith community, and by identifying the core of these strengths, she was able to reach further. Her experiences proved that she was capable, resourceful, and had the necessary drive to succeed in the face of adversity. Florence had been doing the work of a spiritual coach and already had a large client base, she just needed to change the tone and expectations of those interactions. Once she was able to leverage her skills and place a value on her time, a new world of possibilities opened up.

Florence became the business called Florence Brooks Inc. with a portfolio that included The Real Deal and VIP Spiritual Life Coaching as signature products. Both are expressions of her commitment to helping women navigate issues of identity restoration. By putting a premium on her time and natural gifts, she was able to broaden her opportunities and create balance in her own life. With a steady stream of income and better control of her time, Florence is now able to help those less fortunate through The Brooks Family Foundation which supports vulnerable women in underserved communities.

Survival Skills

Dr. Florence Brooks is proof of the limitless capacity of the human spirit and the valuable lessons we can all take from our past experiences, good or bad. In my coaching practice, I often ask my clients, "what would be your survival skill if you found yourself in an unrecognizable place." The answer is often enlightening. For Florence, it was the natural ability to connect with people and inspire. Amid all the talents, passions, and skills, there is a core to each of us, that has been guiding us all along. Once we accept and harness that core and give ourselves permission to value our skills and time, real transformation can occur. This core is the foundation for our personal brand which becomes the platform to expand our sphere of influence and reach our truest potential. A personal brand is not just a goal but an imperative for true growth.

"I couldn't imagine all the wealth I possessed despite and in spite of all I have gone through. I learned I just had to look within myself." – Dr. Florence Brooks

CHAPTER ELEVEN

Getting to Your Core

MULTI-TALENTED PEOPLE ARE usually the most conflicted. They are walking warehouses of opportunities waiting to be fully realized. If only they could figure out where to start!

My coaching practice is replete with exceptionally talented individuals like Florence. They are at all career levels and ages. I have led a group coaching session comprised of a top Wall Street executive, a college student, and a start-up entrepreneur. Despite their range of professional backgrounds and stages in life, their dilemma was the same. They all struggled to channel their wide range of talents into a distinct career path. What they each needed was a way to tell a cohesive career story.

This struggle is one I can relate to. At the beginning of my career, I needed help clarifying latent aspects of my expertise. I had started a social enterprise, connecting American pro-bono consultants with direct fellowship opportunities at African startups. Running this international leadership pipeline program meant I had to wear several professional hats. I was a regular keynote speaker at conferences related to social entrepreneurship, international development, and service. I was a career and transition coach to our fellows who were often uncertain what steps to take next in their careers. I was also the connector for our partners' investment deals. Additionally, I acted as an advisor for our organization to the U.S. State Department and other countries.

This leadership role established me as a thought leader in the world of social entrepreneurship, and yet, I still felt stymied. If only I could synthesize my skills and take it further, I thought. I needed a way to tell a cohesive career story.

Building a personal brand resolved this conundrum for me. Personal branding is the act or process of individuals marketing themselves as businesses. Like Florence, creating one for myself allowed me to fuse my many talents and develop my professional aspirations. I was able to expand my sphere of influence by creating my personal brand, Go Global, Inc., a firm that provides coaching, consulting, impact investing, and leadership strategies. I was now in the position to help business executives and leaders from all spheres of life successfully navigate similar conflicts.

Determine the Core

Coaching some of the most accomplished and ambitious individuals has taught me a lot, but when it comes to determining the core of one's brand and finding one's borderless voice, I've made three key discoveries.

As a multi-talented person, you will be multifaceted. By nature, talented people tend to have more career options. Building one's brand starts with a simple, yet counterintuitive, premise: we are not what we do, what we do is an expression of who we are. Whether you are an entertainer, engineer or entrepreneur, it is imperative to recognize that your roles in life don't define your identity; they are merely an outlet for your personal brand. Making this mental shift made it possible for me to see a larger version of what I could do. Empowered by this shift, I could do more to help others.

The problem is not finding the right talent but your core. Rather than get overwhelmed by the multiplicity of options, finding your core asset will likely be your call to action. During coaching sessions, I ask my clients, "What is your survival skill? What is the one skill you could depend on to support you

outside of your current means of income?"
The answer to this question is the clue to
finding your core.

Then give yourself permission to be a
brand. Conflict persists when you hold yourself back. Creating a personal brand makes it
possible to combine your many talents. Your
expertise can then be developed into products, and from these products, you can build
a portfolio. At this point, your personal brand
is now open for business.

Building Your Brand

Here is a five-step process to build your
personal and professional brand.

1. What is your survival skill and talent?
If you were to be relocated to a new country where you did not have a support network, what skill or talent do you have that
you can rely on to survive? I am not talking
about sophisticated skills required to build

a global business or career. I'm talking about survival. Something to fall back on or help get you back on your feet. Think about basic skills like writing, selling, speaking, organizing, mobilizing, entertaining, and training.

2. **Caption your personal identity in one word.** Getting to the core of your brand starts with being able to identify one word (sometimes two, but not more) that symbolizes your personal identity. Think about it this way: If the labels that define you—your current professional title or even your role as a father, mother or spouse—were suddenly removed, what is the one thing that would still give you a sense of identity and meaning? This could be something for which you have a deep passion or intrinsic insight. Perhaps it's something that comes so naturally that it seems genetically coded as if it were part of your DNA. This could be a cause like "human rights," a core value like "integrity," or perhaps a passion like

my own, which is "connecting" people and ideas.

3. What is your professional identity? Your professional brand is industry-specific and your professional identity is rarely about what you do, but who you are as a leader. It makes no difference if you are entry level or management. Regardless of your current status, a leader by my definition is anyone that solves problems, so if this describes you, you are a leader. Consider the ideal industry for you. Is it non-profit or for-profit? Then think about your sector or niche in this industry. It is a great place to start defining your professional identity. For example, if you are in the reproductive health industry at a nonprofit organization, you may identify as a reproductive health leader or expert.

4. What are your core values? These are a set of guiding principles you live by, and through which you get your sense of moral compass. Like the saying goes, if you stand for nothing, you will fall for anything. Values are the principles you stand for. They constitute the critical components necessary for building your personal brand and finding your voice. Here are some values to explore. Identify the top five that resonate most with you.

Authenticity	Faith	Service
Leadership	Love	Justice
Integrity	Peace	Loyalty
Citizenship	Security	Pleasure
Contribution	Adventure	Wealth
Diversity	Curiosity	Fairness
Learning	Self-Care	Entrepreneurship
Collaboration	Recognition	Independence

5.What is your personal mission statement? Now that you have identified and clarified your personal core values, the last step is to define your personal mission statement. Think about your sense of purpose. Defining it as a statement can seem an overwhelming exercise. However, by considering your core values, you are likely to hit upon the one word that encapsulates your personal identity. Also, consider why these words are important to you and how you see yourself contributing to your immediate environment. The answers will reveal your personal mission statement.

CHAPTER TWELVE

The Impact Investor

Eckhart Tolle, the bestselling author of "The Power of Now," shares a very compelling story as follows:

"A beggar had been sitting by the side of a road for over thirty years. One day a stranger walked by.

'Spare some change?' mumbled the beggar, mechanically holding out his old baseball cap.

'I have nothing to give you,' said the stranger. Then he asked: 'What's that you are sitting on?'

'Nothing,' replied the beggar. 'Just an old

box. I have been sitting on it for as long as I can remember.'

'Ever look inside?' asked the stranger.

'No,' said the beggar. 'What's the point? There's nothing in there.'

'Have a look inside,' insisted the stranger.

The beggar managed to pry open the lid. With astonishment, disbelief, and elation, he saw that the box was filled with gold."

* * *

Conversation creates miracles.

Carrie Rich, whom I met in Rosslyn, Virginia is the founder of Global Good Fund, a unique organization that invests in the leadership development of social entrepreneurs around the world. At the time, she was around 28 years old.

Before I share the incredible story of how Carrie made it happen, I should say she had been active in social change from a young age. If you ask Carrie, she'll say she always had the desire to do something to make the world a better place, even if it meant helping just one person at a time.

Carrie was 14 when she went to Jamaica with a non-profit group called Teens for Technology, which made it possible for her to work with local businesses and teens like herself. In an interview published by Hearts of Fire, Carrie said, "I saw how combining resources, and human capital could have a positive impact on the community and, selfishly, that made me feel good."

Years later, post-college, Carrie met someone who would make a profound difference in her life: her boss. He mentored and coached her and helped her develop into a business leader. She attended business conferences, and at one of them, she met a stranger with whom she conversed with for a while before exchanging business cards. She thought nothing more of it.

Then, on her 26th birthday, her boss made her a proposition. He was going to take her and her friends out to celebrate her birthday. However, if Carrie wanted to use the $100 he was planning to spend for a better purpose, she could have it under one condition: She accomplish something good with it.

Carrie took the money. She contacted six organizations of her favorite non-profit organizations. "If given a thousand dollars," she asked, "what would you do that would have a sustainable impact in your communities?"

Their replies were eye-opening.

"That small amount of money could improve literacy rates in a Washington D.C. classroom," one organization told her.

"That would allow 25 women to graduate from high school in Tanzania," another said.

Carrie had an epiphany. She knew a lot of people. If they all contributed a small amount, it could add up to a great deal of money. With it, Carrie could make an impact doing good in the world. She immediately sent out an email to all her family, friends, and acquaintances. She asked them to make a small donation to her Global Good Fund.

As expected, Carrie received smaller amounts—$5s, $10s, $50s—which added up to larger amounts. She was thrilled. Then, something even more amazing happened. One of the emails was from that stranger she had met years ago at the business conference. She could hardly believe her eyes. "I'd like to send a million dollars," he wrote. He wanted to know where to send the check.

A million dollars?! Carrie thought. Was this for real or was it some kind of prank?

Carrie agreed to meet with him. She chose a public place with surveillance cameras. She arrived early and waited, uncertain what to expect. Would he really show up?

Then he appeared. She was relieved, and then, awestruck when he showed her a cashier's check for $1,000,000!

"What would you do with the money?" he asked.

Carrie had to think fast. She hadn't thought this through, in part, because she hadn't actually expected him to show up. After a moment, she said, "I would identify high potential young leaders around the world, pair them with targeted capital and seasoned executives who have the experience to help grow their leadership development, which would, in turn, grow their businesses and create positive social impact."

Pleased with her response, he handed her the check. It was a moment to remember. Carrie had her first million dollars in hand! The mission of The Global Good Fund was now clear. GGF would identify and invest in the development of young social entrepreneurs around the world who have been working for two years or more in businesses built for social good.

A valuable lesson to learn from here is that a simple conversation with a stranger, which didn't seem notable at the time, actually turned out to be a miracle in the making.

"Can you believe this?" Carrie said, racing back to her boss and tossing the check on the table.

"Yes," he said.

As elated as she was, Carrie started to have doubts. She didn't have money or influence.

She didn't come from a powerful family. "Can I really do this?" she asked.

"Absolutely," he said. With that, he personally matched the million dollars. Again, he had a condition. Carrie would not only start the foundation but, with his support and guidance, she would manage the Board of Directors.

Presto! Overnight, Carrie's Global Good Fund was off to a running start with two million dollars!

Looking back now, Carrie says, "I still pinch myself. A stranger renewed my faith in what strangers can do for each other."

The Global Good Fund pairs emerging entrepreneurs with accomplished executives who share their knowledge and the lessons they have learned, whether they be blunders or achievements.

"It's a win-win," Carrie says. Young social entrepreneurs gain the tutelage they need, and the mentors themselves, while at the peaks of their careers, also get the fulfilling feeling of giving back. They are "living a life of significance," she says.

Give yourself permission

Carrie started without a business plan, website, business license nor office space. All she had was $100 and an email list of friends and family. So how was Carrie Rich able to catapult so immediately from a typical employee to a renowned impact investment leader?

One might argue that she was lucky to have such a great job, mentor, and community. But such a response falls so far from the truth. The real answer lies in the fact that she gave herself permission to determine her own professional identity. She refused to see her present professional status as a limitation.

As an Identity Strategist Coach, I consider myself to be in the business of creating miracle conversations. I speak with individuals about their identity and using methods I have created, allow for transformation to happen.

Time and again, I've seen radical shifts in the ways they see themselves. I start most of my sessions by asking the following question: What is your highest aspiration? During the series of coaching sessions that follow, I challenge them to give themselves permission to embrace the inevitable identity that comes when their vision is realized.

At one of my training workshops that included CEOs, industry leaders, and board members of major U.S. nonprofits and foundations, I asked, "Does anyone describe him or herself as either a professional, entrepreneur, industry or thought leader?" The purpose of this question was to identify with the professional identity that resonated with them most. Surprisingly, despite the caliber of this group, almost everyone identified as either a professional or entrepreneur. Most felt unqualified to be described as industry or thought leaders.

After further inquiry, I found the reason. According to them, their professional identity was not self-defined, it was something defined by others, and which one had to accept.

The scenario above echoes what happens during many of my coaching conversations. Although already accomplished, leaders in career transitions struggle to be the architect of their professional identity and personal brand. Inadvertently, professionals defer this responsibility to their employers and entrepreneurs to their businesses.

They hardly grasped that like other aspects of their identity, their professional identity should not be thrust upon them. One of my most important coaching sessions is a lesson about owning your own power. You are in control. You define your professional identity, not others.

Defining Your Professional Identity

You can define your professional identity through this three-step process:

1. What is your highest professional aspiration? Ask yourself if resources weren't a barrier, what would you envision your career to look like? Think about that dream you've always had, whether it be writing a book, starting a business, or creating a career from your passion. The goal here is not to focus on HOW but to think about WHAT.

2. Who would you become when you accomplish this? Think of a professional title for this aspiration. For example, if you envision owning multiple successful businesses, then consider your role as a serial entrepreneur. If your current reality seems too distant from this new title, that is absolutely fine for now. Keep in mind, however, that your professional identity is how you see yourself, your brand is how the world sees you.

3. What is within your immediate reach that can get you closer to this goal? What is ONE thing you can do right now, that is within your power, to manifest this professional identity? Think about Carrie Rich. Initially, all she could do was contact nonprofits about what they could possibly do with a $1000. Later, she also asked her friends and family for financial donations.

CHAPTER THIRTEEN

The Power of Language

YOUR WORDS CREATE YOUR WORLDS. And your language manifests your dreams. I would explain this concept by sharing two stories.

Amy, one of my coaching clients had long thought about creating arts programs, curating shows, and starting her own business. When we first met, she was completely clueless about how to manifest this dream. She didn't know how to begin, and she didn't trust that she had the skills or motivation to make it happen.

She sat down with me and began to share her dream. We began to meet over the telephone and in person. Here, I challenged the words she uses to describe herself, even though she was she was still in a phase of transition. Then during one of our conversations, she had what initially seemed like a small miracle moment. We were talking about the concepts of survival skills, achievements, telling one's story from a forward-looking perspective. When she realized that there were small adjustments she could make right away that would allow her to manifest her dreams in tangible ways.

She instantly changed how she thought about herself, speaking her dreams into reality. As a result of her new strategy, one month after she started getting coaching, she proposed a show to a major arts center in her city and it was accepted. After that, she had no choice but to take herself seriously and to believe that she had what it took to become an entrepreneur.

Amy shared with me, "For a long time, I told people I was an aspiring curator. Then after our coaching sessions, I started telling people I AM a curator. Just making that small switch completely changed the way I introduced myself, thought about my goals and I noticed it changed how people saw me. On my business card and on my social accounts I call myself a 'creative economy catalyst' to sum up all the different roles I fill in my professional life."

* * *

I also had a similar experience with my coach. This is my story:

Like many other leaders, I found my calling in college where I chose a nonprofit leadership path. I started a nonprofit preparing my fellow students for the real world but I still came out of school feeling confused. Now in hindsight I would say I was in a state of professional identity crisis. I was at a crossroads wondering whether I should continue the route I had started on or cross over to the business world. At this height of this dilemma, I resorted to taking some time for introspection.

My Aha moment came watching an interview on TV with thought leader Ndidi Nweleli. It was a very unbelievable experience because I now suddenly saw this woman who was so eloquently expressing ideas I've been contemplating for years but didn't have the right language to articulate. The more she spoke the more I became convinced that I would have to do all I could to connect with her.

A few weeks later she was scheduled to speak at a conference, and I made it my goal to attend and try my best to speak with her there. Getting there wasn't easy. I was the last person to register for the event. Because I wasn't working and had taking time off for introspection, it was a miracle to get the money for the conference together. In fact, they wouldn't let me in at first, my name could not be found on the registration list. I had to negotiate my way to get it.

Right as she was getting off the platform after giving her presentation, I defiantly walked towards the platform to thank her for such a great presentation. I immediately cut to the chase stating, "Ma'am, I came to this conference just to have the opportunity to speak with you"

She responded kindly, "That's interesting, how can I be of help?"

Without further delay, I said, "I want you to be my life coach."

My turning point came in our very first coaching session. "If you want to make money and still help people then you are a social entrepreneur," she said. These words were life-changing. That defining moment became my opportunity of having a mentor figure come into my life to help crystalize my professional identity. Although prior to this conversation, I never heard the word *Social Entrepreneur*, in six months after that meeting, I had all I needed to be the architect of the opportunities I was seeking.

Because my paradigm of myself has been altered and I am now able to rightly articulate my professional identity, I started seeing opportunities (that have always been around me) like never before. It was easy to give myself permission to reach for my dreams. I applied to what was at the time one of the most competitive opportunities in my field. I won a global business plan competition that changed my life. It was sponsored by Microsoft Unlimited Potential, the social division of the Microsoft Corporation.

It was a search for 100 young social entrepreneurs from around the world with ideas that have the potential to change the world. This program gave my first global stage and network of investors, partners and thought leaders. This breakthrough was the beginning of the rest of my story as a leader in the field of social enterprise. Shortly after that I joined the United Nations as a consultant and came to the United States to work in a State Department program for international nonprofit leaders. All that was made possible because of a conversation I determined to have with a coach who changed the language with which I told my story.

Today, I have the same conversation I had with my coach with leaders at all levels in a state of professional identity transition. Through these conversations, they crystallize their true professional identity, and in turn are able to reach for their highest aspirations. After telling this story at one of my speaking events in San Francisco, California, one of the attendees walked up to me and said, "That conversation was a miracle".

Had that conversation not happened when it did, I might still be mired down in my professional identity crisis, trying to find clarity for a career path that brought me meaning and purpose.

CHAPTER FOURTEEN

The Power of Identity

NOW THAT YOU HAVE an idea of your professional identity, let us look at some advantages that come with your newly found clarity:

New Opportunities – A significant number of my international clients come to me through social media with little, if any, marketing efforts on my part. A client from Australia says she found me by simply typing the keywords "Identity Strategist" on the LinkedIn platform. When it comes to creating new opportunities, there is a direct correlation between the thoughtfulness and intentionality you have regarding your professional identity. Headhunters are routinely seeking qualified candidates on the LinkedIn platform. These can be for six – or seven-figure opportunities. Because jobs at higher levels are rarely advertised, the keywords that capture your professional identity on LinkedIn and other platforms will either filter you in or out from such opportunities.

Industry leadership – We all aspire to reach the highest echelons of our careers, but without a clear professional identity strategy, the road to the top is a longer, and possibly serpentine commute. A clear professional identity is an articulation of what success looks like, and how, exactly, to get there. The right professional identity strategy will enable you to accelerate the journey to become a recognized leader in your industry and field.

Specialization – Today's competitive job

market favors the specialist and not the generalist. The world of marketing, for instance, has several areas of specialization such as co-branding, cause marketing, tele-marketing, social media marketing, direct marketing, and so on. Being deliberate and strategic with your professional identity will increase your chances to own a market niche, and dominate a new market space of limited competition and vast opportunities.

Personal brand – I would describe personal branding as the difference between renting versus owning real estate. The owners gain home equity, whereas the renters do not. Your professional identity can grow to become a personal brand that garners brand equity that can be monetized. It is almost impossible to build a personal brand without first defining one's professional identity. Again, your personal brand is the way the world sees you, whereas your professional identity is the way you see yourself.

Storytelling – Without a crystal-clear picture of your professional identity, you cannot tell your story. This is crucial for jobs and business opportunities. Stories give you the power to positively influence your audience. In my storytelling workshops, I coach corporate leaders and business owners on the inseparability of their story and their identity. I take it further to indicate that storytelling is not one's past to date, rather it's one's proximity to one's dreams. True storytelling is an act of creation. It is the opportunity to bring your dreams within your reach, and to inspire your audience to co-create with you. When you tell your true story, you set in motion a conversation that creates miracles.

CHAPTER FIFTEEN

The Advocate

When you engage in work that taps your talent and fuels your passion — that rises out of a great need in the world that you feel drawn by conscience to meet — therein lies your voice, your calling, your soul's code.

— The 8th Habit, Stephen Covey

A CRISIS IS A TERRIBLE THING TO WASTE. It may seem terrible in the moment but it may also be opportunities in the making, disguised as challenges. One of my coaching clients, Deb Marcano, is a good case study of this point.

Deb was having a bad year. She was having relationship troubles and working at a job she didn't like. What's worse is that she had recently received a medical diagnosis for an illness that had the possibility of being terminal.

She had so many dreams, but with this new diagnosis, everything suddenly seemed out of reach. She loved acting and photography, and from the time she was a child, she had fantasized about having a large family. In an act of desperation and looking for inspiration, she boarded a plane and flew to Lalibela, Ethiopia.

Lalibela is considered one of the most spiritual places in the world. It is known for its monolithic churches, a group of eleven structures chiseled from live volcanic rock more than 900 years ago. In terms of architectural scale, size and sophistication, there are no man-made structures like them anywhere in the world. Located in the Amhara region of

Ethiopia, the small town attracts thousands of pilgrims and tourists every year.

Deb was surprised by what she found in Lalibela. The towering underground churches impressed her, but what struck her more was the abject poverty and living conditions of the locals in the city. Deb struggled to understand how tourists, with as much as they had, could ignore the suffering of the locals around them.

Deb walked through town. Looking into the beggar's faces, she couldn't help thinking, "That could be me." She came across two young girls with whom she felt immediately drawn. The children felt a connection with her as well. Deb talked with them for hours. Eventually, they led her home to their mother. Not only were the two women around the same age, they also looked a lot alike. The family welcomed Deb, and the girls' mother even performed the traditional Ethiopian coffee ceremony. Moved by their hospitality and the ease with which they bonded, Deb agreed to stay in touch.

Meeting this family changed Deb. Before going to Lalibela, she said, "I took photos to show people what a place was like." After, however, her worldview had changed. "I wanted people to see that there are not just churches here. There are people here. I wanted to make a difference with my work now. I didn't just want to show beautiful pictures."

The connection to this family, and consequently, a shift in perspective, became the impetus for many changes in her life. When she returned to New York from her trip, she focused on photography and started working in the nonprofit world. She continued to write to the family. Several years and many letters later, Deb learned the mother of the girls had suddenly died. Deb unofficially "adopted" the family, supporting them financially. She wired money every month for more than 10 years. Her support saw the children through their schooling, the start of their new families and then their businesses.

"I have been the mother of these children longer than their biological parents have," said Deb. Eager to see them after so many years apart, she returned to Lalibela. During her visit, she photographed some of the residents. The images from this series of work have been displayed in galleries across the United States, including Portland, Oregon, California, and New York. They have also appeared in several online journals.

I met Deb at one of my Tell Your Story events in New York. During these workshops, I coached individuals on how to use storytelling to transform challenging episodes into life-changing opportunities. At Tell Your Story, Deb shared her Lalibela experience with me. She wanted to expand her impact beyond this particular family to the entire Lalibela community. She was already a professional photographer involved with numerous nonprofit organizations, but she was unsure how to take things further with her career.

What Deb didn't realize was that a path had already emerged. The challenges she had faced—and overcome—had inadvertently propelled her toward realizing her ultimate aspirations. During our coaching sessions, she learned how to embrace the story of her journey as her life's purpose. Then, the real work began. She created Lalibela Living, a documentary series that promotes what Deb has coined as "transformational tourism" to Lalibela. Since then, Deb and I have teamed up to co-host several Tell Your Story events in different parts of the country.

This year Deb will also be launching The Marcano Foundation, a philanthropic initiative dedicated to supporting the disadvantaged families of Lalibela. Nineteen years after her first trip there, Deb has transformed herself from an unhappy and unhealthy, lost individual with unrealized dreams into a devoted mother and an art-repreneur. She has become one of Lalibela's greatest advocates.

CHAPTER SIXTEEN

The Power of Moments

Exhaust the little moment. Soon it dies.
And be it gash or gold it will not come
Again in this identical disguise.

— *Gwendolyn Brooks, Annie Allen*

Crisis moments

I CAN'T SAY IT ENOUGH: a crisis is a terrible thing to waste. Life-changing opportunities often masquerade as crises. Talking about the transformative power of crisis, I would like you to consider the story about Susan G. Komen, a woman who lost her battle to breast cancer, and whose name might otherwise also be lost if it were not for the promise of a beloved sister.

In 1980, after her sister's long struggle with breast cancer, Nancy G. Brinker made a declaration that she would do everything in her power to end breast cancer "forever." With a shoebox containing $200 and a list of potential donor names, the Susan G. Komen organization came into being. Today, it is the world's largest nonprofit source of funding for the fight against breast cancer. According to the Susan G. Komen® organization, it funds more than $2.9 billion in groundbreaking research, community health outreach, advocacy and programs in more than 60 countries.

I shared this story at one of my story coaching intensives. Days later, one of the participants, a woman named Robin Baker, came back to me with her own experience, which was in some ways similar to the Susan G. Komen story. During her sophomore year of college, her mother was diagnosed with inflammatory breast cancer. In the midst of her mother's battle, during Robin's junior year, her father unexpectedly passed away. Then, during her senior year, Robin's mother was transitioned to hospice care. She was dying.

"That day, she made me promise that I would take care of my then 14-year-old brother," Robin recounted. "And that I would live a life of service and aid in improving the lives of people in Liberia, her come country."

Six months after Robin's father's death, and two weeks after this particular conversation with her mother, Robin's mother lost her battle with breast cancer. "I watched my mother, a phenomenally strong woman, and provider, turn fragile and helpless," Robin now shares. "During her final days, she requested that family allow her to perform simple activities such as grooming, bathing and dressing independently. She found such joy, dignity, and fulfillment performing these simple tasks. These memories prompted me to change my career interest from athletic training to occupational therapy, a profession that helps people across their lifespan do the things they want and need to do regardless of injury or illness."

At that point in time, however, Robin had missed all the official deadlines to apply for graduate school. She could have deferred her decision for a year, but instead, she contacted Howard University to ask about applying late to the program. Robin's request was not only approved, but she was accepted into the program. Without financial aid or even a solid plan, she moved from North Carolina to Maryland. At Howard University, she pursued a Master of Science in occupational therapy.

One year into her master's program, at the age of 21, Robin took on the responsibility of becoming the legal guardian of her then 15-year-old brother. This period during graduate school was one of the most trying and depressed periods of her life, however, she had made a promise to her mother that she was determined to fulfill.

Robin completed her clinical rotation for her graduate program in San Jose, Costa Rica. This experience changed the trajectory of her life. It sparked her interest in the intersection between global health, disability, and rehabilitation. It was in Costa Rica where Robin's love for her profession and love for her mother would germinate into the legacy that would one day become GoTHERAPY.

With my coaching strategies, Robin transformed her crisis into a path determining her borderless voice. Robin had already had a life-changing experience before she met me, but now, she seized upon the opportunity to form a new narrative out of it. Today, GoTHERAPY has grown to provide rehabilitation services for people with disabilities in the United States, Liberia, and Ghana. Through GoTHERAPY, she not only fulfills the promise to her mother, she is now creating a legacy and global impact of her own.

What crisis are you wasting? A crisis is by nature life-altering, intrusive and tragic. However, as I've pointed out, embedded within these moments are seeds to transformative opportunities. In my experience helping individuals like Robin tell their story, I've witnessed that stories that come from crises are often the most compelling and influential. Such stories are pathways to one's purpose, legacy, and identity.

A Crisis can be a gift when you know the right course of action but lack the mental fortitude to take such action, thus delaying the pursuit of your dream. These moments show up as the loss of a job, the demise of a dream, or even personal or professional failure, which can occur on an epic scale. Most of the time, such experiences are beyond our control. For many, the problem is not so much the crisis itself, but the resulting missed opportunity of not forming a narrative out of it. What has happened has happened, but what matters ultimately is what you do about it. Embrace your crisis moment as your life's work and story.

Defining Moment

A key component of telling your story is the defining moment. To illustrate this concept, consider the history of Starbucks, the world leader in coffee. In the beginning, Starbucks started as a small startup enterprise out of Seattle, Washington. Its core business was not coffee in paper cups as we know today but selling coffee beans.

Howard Schultze, the co-founder of Starbucks, discovered during a visit to Italy that coffee could be more than a hot caffeinated drink in a paper cup. He realized it could be an experience. This was a defining moment. Upon his return, he seized on the possibility of elevating the core business by creating a communal component, a unique coffee experience that existed outside of the home and office.

This transformation redefined the identity of Starbucks to what it is today. Not only is it a household name, but it is a major fiber of American daily life. Schultze took what he experienced from a cafe in Italy and reinvented coffee drinking, making it the staple it is today, not only in the U.S. but around the world.

What defining moments in your story are you wasting? It may be good or bad, tragic or inspirational, perhaps random or even deliberate. Your defining moment is the blueprint for potential professional and business opportunities.

"All the world is full of suffering. It is also full of overcoming." — Helen Keller

Finding Your Defining Moment

To show you exactly how to discover this moment and make a compelling story out of it, here is my challenge. Think about your story. Let go of the "enoughs" for the moment. It's neither good enough, nor not good enough. For now, it is just a story. Your story.

Now, recall a defining moment in your

story; an Aha! moment, a turning point, or moment of truth. This is a moment when things suddenly came into perspective for you. It could be, as it was with Carrie, a conversation with a mentor or boss, or as with Deb in Lalibela or like Sandra a moment of heightened awareness. Or, it could be a similar experience to my own, which occurred in a place one might least expect, an airport.

Focus on this moment. Allow yourself to relive the experience in your mind. This is your defining moment. Where do you feel it in your body? Does remembering the moment bring any emotions with it? Focus on those feelings. Embrace the experience and make a new story out of this.

Peak Moments

One's yearning for purpose and pursuit of identity is not just personal but universal. Whether you work in business or engineering, are an investor, or a social worker, you are part of the millions globally who seek meaning in their occupation. The ancient question, "Why am I here?" will in all likelihood exist until the end of time. Meaning rarely includes the numbers in your bank account unless you are using that account to do something purposeful for others. If you read the biographies of successful people you will notice that without fail they talk about how their lives changed when they found meaning.

I believe the answer to this question may also lie in another question: "What are you most passionate about?" Even as simple as this question appears, I find that it's a struggle for most people to answer. If you can't identify a passion, then ask yourself, if someone gave you a month to do whatever you wanted to do (and you were paid for doing it) what would you do? I find that when I ask people about their passion, or even about what they would like to do if they could, that part of their paradigm that says, "No one gets paid to have fun," kicks in. When they identify a passion the next thought is, "You can't make a living doing that." And they simply exclude that activity as a possibility.

They fail to identify their passion and instead eliminate it as an "unreasonable" daydream. As I mentioned earlier, multi-talented people often struggle the most. The burden to sift through their numerous interests and opportunities often leaves them in a state of confusion, perhaps even conflict. Don't fret if you recognize yourself to be in this category. Recognize you are not alone. The fact that you are aware of the need for meaning is already a step in the right direction. A LinkedIn survey of 8,000 professionals found that one in four US professionals and 30% of global workers say they earn a living from their childhood dream job or a related field.

Now, target what you are most passionate about using this three-step process:

1. *"Don't worry about what the world needs.*

Ask what makes you come alive and do that. Because what the world needs are people who have come alive." –Howard Thurman

When was the time in your life you felt most alive? Think about moments when you felt fulfilled by what you were doing, or occasions that felt deeply meaningful. They do not have to be moments where others saw or thought the event was meaningful. These are moments you felt satisfied, or as though your actions, your presence, or your words or encouragement made a difference. This could be a time where you were on your way to a project and felt deep within yourself that you just "knew" you were in the right place at the right time and good things were happening or going to happen.

2. When were the peak moments of your career?

"Everything that happens to you is your teacher. The secret is to sit at the feet of your own life and be taught by it." –Polly B. Berends

Don't just think about the times you were successful, or won an award, or were noticed by your supervisors. The goal here is to identify your sense of aliveness while at work, or perhaps moments that feel or felt most meaningful while you were doing something you particularly enjoyed about your job. Maybe you were able to troubleshoot a problem or fix a piece of broken machinery no one else could. Maybe you intuitively grasped the solution to a long-standing problem. The project itself doesn't have to be something you feel passionately about, what matters is your feeling of meaning and fulfillment at the moment. If you are a teacher, such a moment might mean when a student succeeded and returned to share their success with you, crediting what they learned from you as part of their reason for success. Perhaps things you have learned and passed along to others through your work have inspired them. Are you a mentor? Have your mentoring efforts been rewarding? Think of a time, or an event where you embraced your career decision for some reason.

3. What were the peak moments of your career? *"Failure's hard, but success is far more dangerous. If you're successful at the wrong thing, the mix of praise and money and opportunity can lock you in forever." –Bridget Bradley Gray"*

The answers you get to those first two questions are what I refer to as your "peak experiences." A **peak experience** is a moment accompanied by a euphoric mental state often achieved by self-actualizing individuals. Peak experiences were originally described by psychologist Abraham Maslow as "moments of highest happiness and fulfillment" in his 1964 work *Religions, Values, and Peak Experiences*. They are considered to be so profound and emotionally uplifting that many describe them as "religious" in nature. They aren't just moments in which you feel happy, but moments where you feel or sense an extremely intense connection with your purpose and work, and the moment. The moment doesn't need to be earth-shattering in reality. It just has to affect you deeply.

Peak Moments should not be confused with **Defining Moments.** A defining moment is a point in your life when you're urged to make a pivotal or critical decision about your next step, or when you experience something that fundamentally changes you. It's a time when your essential nature is revealed in the moment of an event. Not only do these moments define us, but they transform our perceptions and ultimately our behaviors. Think of when Howard Schultze realized coffee wasn't just a product, but an experience.

Defining Moments can happen anytime, anywhere, and are in general life moments. They can reference something about your career, but they radically alter your paradigms.

Peak Moments are generally career-specific in that they play an important role in working towards self-actualization. Self-actualization is actually considered quite rare, which means that peak experiences can be equally elusive. Some surveys show people reported that peak experiences tended to occur during professional, artistic, athletic or religious experiences.

Once you have identified your peak moments, the last step is to consider what positive qualities you bring to this work and which skill sets you will need to utilize. It is possible to do this on your own, although working with a mentor, a coach, or someone who knows how to walk you down this path can not only be more productive, but faster — freeing you up to take advantage of your new insights.

CHAPTER SEVENTEEN

Monetizing the Moments

What makes you unique,
makes you successful.

—*William Arruda, Career Distinction*

TO MONETIZE YOUR STORY and brand, you want to create an economic machine for your voice. By this, I mean expanding your influence, impact, and income beyond your current reality. As Marianne Williamson once said, "As we let our lights shine, we unconsciously give other people permission to do the same. As we're liberated from our own fear, our presence automatically liberates others."

Now to explore some strategies for establishing a monetary (and non-monetary) value for the unique contributions you bring to the world:

10 Monetization Strategies

1. Serve with your skills. Monetization is the process of establishing a monetary value for anything. Another word for this exchange is *sales* which I refer to as *serve*. I understand that not everyone likes the idea of selling or fundraising. But I would like to offer you an alternate perspective. Question, do you like to *help* people, and do you like to serve? What if I tell you helping people, selling, and serving are all the same thing? To put this into a clearer perspective – remember the last time you were at your favorite restaurant. While you were waiting, can you remember being asked the question,

"Have you been served?" Chances are they "served" you so well, that you ended up leaving a generous tip behind in addition to whatever the check was. This explains my point – serving is nothing but an exchange for a monetary and non-monetary value.

2. Become a content creator. "Content is King." In his 1996 essay Bill Gates writes, *"Content is where I expect much of the real money will be made on the Internet".* In this information age, you are either a content creator or a content consumer, period. To monetize your brand, you will have to create, distribute and exchange your content for monetary value. If you are finding it hard to create content, go back to the peak moments exercise. There, you will find milestones in your career where you experienced moments of aliveness. In these moments are contents to be monetized. For example, one of my peak moments was when I received an unexpected call from a friend asking me, "How much do you charge for life coaching?" At that time, I didn't know what a life coach was and that I was already doing that work. As far as I was concerned, I was a professional development speaker and trainer. That call made me realize that I had content I had garnered over the years from my professional development and it could be monetized as life coaching training as well.

3. Become a product creator. It is my experience in working with skilled and talented professionals that they struggle to distill their vast experience and know-how into products and services that can be monetized. As an excuse for this, they would rather remain pro bono consultants rather them give themselves permission to create and test out their products in the marketplace. This is what I tell them, and I will tell you the same—you will have to trust in the *generosity of the marketplace*—it will tell you what you are doing right and what you can improve upon. This is called prototyping or ideation. At this stage, what you need is an MVP – Minimum Viable

Product. It does not have to perfect. Again, the generosity of the marketplace will be to perfect the process and furnish you with all the information that you need to monetize your product or service.

4. Become a story collection agent. Not so much in the literal sense of being a collection agent, by this, I mean becoming adept at collecting stories. Both yours; your defining and peaks moments as well as the ones happening around you. As a business, you should have a system for collecting success stories from your clients. Tell these stories on a page on your website called Success Stories or Testimonials. The same also applies to you as a solo entrepreneur or professional. Your LinkedIn or personal website should have the stories of those clients or customers who have experienced your work and services. This builds your credibility and multiplies your promotional efforts which will ultimately result in monetization opportunities.

5. Put a premium on your time. By establishing an hourly rate for your expertise, you will be amazed at how fast you will be able to grow your brand as an expert and thought leader in your field. I was speaking about this concept at one of my events, and someone countered by saying, "I do regard myself as a thought-leader but I just don't like charging for my time". My response was, "We really don't know if your "clients" think you are a leader or not." Obviously, he was taken aback by my response, but I went on to explain that the standards are a lot higher when clients are paying for your services versus when they aren't. Secondly, you can't give what you don't have. The more you have, the more of your time and expertise you can give. The story of Florence, the spiritual coach is a good case for this.

6. Seek speaking opportunities. One of my coaching clients is an award-winning author who took significant time off from her work to start a family. Given the gap in her work experience, she was having a difficult time returning and picking up where she left off. The first thing I did was to get to her core passion and to ask her why she writes. Then I asked her to amplify this passion by creating a speaking component as a part of her brand. Because her professional identity was a writer, she struggled to see herself as a speaker, but finally, she did. She started by creating a workshop on creative writing, *her passion*, which was immediately sold out because of her authority as a published author. That is what speaking opportunities do for your expertise, they amplify the circle of impact, influence, and income for your core competence. So, consider finding or creating a speaking platform for your expertise, and you will be amazed at how many monetization opportunities will follow.

7. Endorse complementary products. Your story allows you to activate your tribe; a community of like-minded individuals.

Because of this, you can endorse messages, products, and services that are complementary to your brand to this community. You can do this online with your social media network or with mailing lists as well as offline at your events or joint venture with established brands. Often, we think that it is only celebrities or influencers with thousands of followers that have the power to endorse corporate brands. Anyone can endorse a brand, if you have a tribe. Telling your story will allow you to build this community and establishing your brand identity.

8. Expand your community impact. What is your leadership role in your community? Whatever this role is, consider ways to stretch the impact you are currently having even further. At one of my coaching sessions, a client was so moved by this idea that he researched the current priorities and vision of the Mayor of his State. Then he reached out to key government officials to see how he could make a difference at a state level. Consider joining a local non-profit, starting one, or volunteering at an existing program to expand your community impact.

9. Expand your international impact. How would you identify outside of your home country? Whatever your impact in the community is or whatever the work you do professionally, this is your international identity. People typically identify internationally as either as a permanent or temporary resident, visitor or tourist. You change this identity for yourself and give yourself permission to expand your local impact internationally and manifest the identity of a global leader.

10. Open your brand for business. The last and final step is to launch your personal brand on social media platforms and your personal website. On your website or social media, consider creating a page where you list what you offer, and how people can reach you to learn more. Within a few months, after I opened my personal website for business, I received an inquiry from the World Bank offering to hire me as a speaker for a storytelling workshop for business leaders around the world. This can be your story too when you decide to tell your story and take authority over your brand identity.

***

Congratulations! You've made it. Chances are one, or possibly more, of the stories and strategies in this book resonated with you. If you haven't yet, you are on the verge of unleashing your borderless voice.

Finding your voice, your story puts you in the position to inspire others around you to find theirs as well. In turn, you will also establish a monetary (and non-monetary) value for the unique contributions you bring to the world.

Thank you for this opportunity to share

some insights with you through the pages of this book. Nothing pleases me more than to help you discover your defining moments, recognize your powerful story, and ultimately, acknowledge the reach of your borderless voice. I look forward to hearing about how you've been able to put this book to work, and just as importantly, hearing your stories and what your new and borderless voice sounds like.

ABOUT THE AUTHOR

Gbenga is a West African word that means Elevate.

As a social entrepreneur, impact investor, and identity strategist, Gbenga applies his wealth of experience in social enterprise, philanthropy and international service as a bridge builder – bridging the gap of access holding back leaders from making imprints on the global stage.

Today, as an identity strategist, Gbenga architects the personal brand of leaders at all levels in career transition. He has coached hundreds of business and nonprofit leaders at organizations like Verizon, Airbnb, American Express, Teach for America, The Foundation Center, Susan G Komen and UN Foundation. Gbenga's international platforms include the Social Enterprise World Forum, and his Tell Your Story Series has reached business leaders across the corporate world.

Gbenga regularly works with the governmental agencies in the United States and in several emerging market countries to empower profit and nonprofit leaders. He has received global recognition for his work and impact. He is proudly an Atlas Corps Alum, United States, Global Young Social Entrepreneurs Fellow, Malaysia and Cordes / Opportunity Collaboration Fellow, Mexico. Gbenga writes on identity and professional development for *The Huffington Post* and makes his impact investments through The GO Foundation and LDI Africa. Gbenga also serves as an Advisor to the Global Health Corps, an international nonprofit that mobilizes a global community of emerging leaders to build the movement for health equity.

For more information about Gbenga or to be in touch, visit www.gbenga.org

Made in the USA
Middletown, DE
25 May 2019